GET YOUR
HANDS
OFF MY BUTT

*The Hands-On Guide to Avoiding the
Welfare System*

THE BRILLIONAIRE

GET YOUR
HANDS
OFF MY BUTT
*The Hands-On Guide to Avoiding the
Welfare System*

_____

Authored by
RW Jones

Contributions Made By Charles M. Griffin

Published by Can I Live, Inc
PO Box 25502 | Alexandria VA 22313 | 202.996.0880 | www.canilive.org

Can I Live, Inc is committed to excellence, accountability and personal responsibility. The company reflects the philosophy established by its founder, based on Proverbs 29:2,

"When the Righteous are in Authority, the People Rejoice, But When the Wicked Rule, the People Mourn."

Book Cover Design by Elton Benjamin

Researched by Kelvin Spragley

Technical Assistance and Editing by Charles Griffin –Griffin Global Enterprises

Published in the United States of

America ISBN: 978-0-9855498-4-8
1. Family & Relationships / Parenting / Single Parent
2. Self-Help / Personal Growth /
General 14.09.22

TABLE OF CONTENTS

*This book is dedicated
to every struggle, every pain, every lie, every betrayal,
rejection, abandonment, evil intent, and every harmful
attempt on my life; every opportunity people took to
take what was of value, precious, protected and sacred;
every stolen concept, plan, program and idea that I
diligently labored for.
For every wrong; through Love, it is made right.*

Preface

Why This Handbook for Women

In reviewing current statistics that tell the story about life for teenagers and young adult women, an alarm went off in my head. It's time to rock out ladies. It's time to confront the threats of low educational attainment, poverty, unplanned pregnancy, single-family homes and sexually transmitted diseases.

To secure our futures and the futures of our children we must make education and pursuing God's purpose a priority in our lives. We must diligently pursue productive pathways, avoid unplanned and unwed pregnancies at all costs, and protect ourselves against sexually transmitted diseases, and decisions that foster dependency.

Let me share some alarming stats with you:

Teenage Pregnancy[1]

- 80 percent of teenage pregnancies are unintended
- The main rise in the teen pregnancy rate is among girls younger than 15
- Close to 25 percent of teen mothers have a second child within two years of the first birth
- Sons of teenage mothers have a 13 percent greater chance of ending up in prison as compared to their peers

Sexually Transmitted Diseases[1]

- At least one in every four teenage girls nationwide has a sexually transmitted disease
- Half of all new HIV infections occur in teenagers
- About 66% of all sexually transmitted diseases (STDs) occur in people 25 years of age or younger

Education

- By age 30, only 1.5 percent of women who had pregnancies as a teenager have a college degree[1]
- Individuals who attain a bachelor's degree make over a million dollars more over the course of their lives than those who do not [2]

Poverty

- Over 29.9% of single mothers live below poverty[3]
- Children living in single female-headed families were more than four times as likely to live in poverty, and seven times as likely to live in deep poverty than children living in married couple families[3]
- Children from low income families were twice as likely to suffer from ADHD[4]

Depression/ Self-esteem

- Women suffer from depression at a rate twice as high as men[5]
- Thirty-seven percent (37%) of women had suffered significant physical or sexual abuse by the age of 21[6]

1. The National Campaign to Prevent Teen Pregnancy. Facts and Stats.Thenationalcampaign.org.

2. U.S. Department of Commerce Economics and Statistics Administration: Bureau of the Census. More Education Means Higher Career Earnings. Census.gov. August 1994.

3. U.S. Census Bureau. People and Families in Poverty by Selected Characteristics: 2009 and 2010. Census.gov.

4. Exposure to Gestational Diabetes Mellitus and Low Socioeconomic Status: Effects on Neurocognitive Development and Risk of Attention-Deficit/Hyperactivity Disorder in Offspring by: Yoko Nomura, PhD, MPH; David J. Marks, PhD; Bella Grossman, MA; Michelle Yoon, BS, BA; Holly Loudon, MD, MPH; Joanne Stone, MD; Jeffrey M. Halperin, PhD.

5. American psychological Association. Research Agenda for Psychosocial and Behavioral Factors in Women's Health.

6. Women's Depression Rate Is Higher. Nytimes.com. [Online] December 6, 1990.

Background
The Story Behind The Story

If you haven't heard my story, I will give you the short version. Twenty years ago, I found myself pregnant with a child from a man I thought I would marry. I would tell the man of my dreams almost every day that God either sent him in my life or will use him to benefit me–either way I would win in the end. He never understood why I would say those exact words to him almost daily. At the time, I did not know what would become of our relationship, but whatever it was, it would be great. Needless to say, this man gave me my first son and was a direct connection to the doors of destiny for my life. He worked in a juvenile facility and was able to get me a job working as a youth counselor. It was there that I found the fruit of a problem that I was created to solve. Notice, I said the fruit. It has taken me thirteen (13) years of education and hundreds of thousands of dollars in student loan debt to get to the root of the issue–but that is the subject of another book.

So here I am working in this secure juvenile facility where we had in our care one hundred-sixty (160) young females who were sentenced there for committing some offense. I noticed that out of one hundred-sixty (160) girls, one hundred-fifty-eight (158) of them were African American who lived with a single mom. None knew their dads and they all were high school dropouts. I thought, "NO way is this an accident!" My antennas went up and I knew there was something going on that was the result of a common, systemic problem in society.

I was compelled, and I mean seriously compelled, to solve this problem. The first place I decided to go for answers was the classroom. I enrolled in school as a criminal justice major looking to save these young girls. The questions I asked could not be answered on that level and so I knew very early on that this journey would be a very long one. I was enrolled in a local community college as a single mother and having major issues making ends meet therefore, I went to the department of social services. They told me I had to come out of school in order for them to help me. They would pay for me to get a CNA (Certified Nurse's Assistant) certificate, but not a criminal justice, political science or law degree. So, I did what any woman in her RIGHT mind would have done. I stayed in school and decided that this was the road I would have to take because it was not just about me. I had one hundred-sixty (160) girls to save. Before I could get a full year under my belt, I got pregnant for the second time. I thought okay this was not the plan, but in fact I had no real plan. You have heard people say that if you fail to plan then you plan to fail. Well, I had clearly failed to plan, but I knew for sure that failing was not an option for me. I had to do something to make a change for my future.

In school, struggling as a single mother, I thought things could not get any worse until I found myself pregnant again. No way, I thought to myself. I am blaming everyone for my mistakes. I blamed the devil's temptation for my transgressions until one day a pastor of a church said it's not the devil, it's you. That was my sobering moment. But not sobering enough until I found myself pregnant again. That's right I said it, pregnant again for the fourth time. It took me five years to complete a two-year degree. I was trying to solve a problem that I was becoming. So, I am the woman who knows firsthand about child support, welfare, court and drama. I was the young female pursuing the woman of my dreams.

I was able to earn my Associate's degree in Criminal Justice, Bachelor's degree in Politics, Economics and Law and a Master's degree in Public Administration. This book and the others that will come are only the beginning of me coming back to save those young girls who are now adult women. The sad part of it all is that most of the youth detention centers, jails and other secure facilities across the United States are filled with Black youth. I believe that it is our duty to do more to make sure that Black youth, like all other youth have the parenting and support they need to be healthy, productive citizens.

So now you have the cliff notes version of how I got to this place. I shared my story with you to let you know that I am here with you in the trenches, in the hustle and grind but on the other side. The grind is much different on this side; however, I hope to help some of you make that transition.

INTRODUCTION
Your Secret Garden

This book is designed to reach all females exactly where they are and guide them to where they want to be in life–personally and professionally. This is a not a chick circuit book designed to bash men and glorify women. This book takes a light, but intellectual approach to encouraging women to be the best they can be in academia, in their personal lives, in their careers, and as parents.

Everyone is constantly looking at women to produce, looking to us for answers to problems in society, but because many of us are looking for ways to make our personal situations better, we stare back with blank faces. Many of us are so caught in our struggles and destructive behavior patterns that we find trouble creating a better way for ourselves and ultimately contribute to the problems. For those of you trying to find your way and for those of you who feel trapped in your circumstances, I have a few words for you–live your life as a story being told. Understanding that you are the main character starring in your own lifetime movie; it is up to you to write each scene. Don't walk to this new life–run! Run like your life depended on it. Don't run blindly but run with a plan in your hand. In this book you will find an easy blueprint to follow to help you to a new and brighter future for yourself.

Women often deal with so much nonsense and unnecessary drama. We have to grow to have zero tolerance for the drama! We must see past all the smoke and mirrors and not be easily impressed with the ways of the world that would lead us to degrade ourselves and accept things that we don't want. We must learn to love more discreetly and love best those who love us. When we start with the love within, we love ourselves better and force others to do the same.

Have you ever thought, "Why me?" The answer is another question, "If not you, then who?" Everything you have gone through was to make you a better person so that you would better serve, not yourself, but others.

I speak to the vision inside of you that is dying to come out. Let this book be the seed that will produce a harvest that is greater than all you can think or imagine.

The nation is in a state of emergency in the face of economic disparities, violence, lack of education, drug abuse, racism, the degradation of the woman and children, and the prevalence of single-parent homes. Throughout our history in America, the woman has served as a hero to the family and pillar to the community. That strength, resilience and hope you can find nowhere except in a people who rely not on themselves but on a higher source. I have found this spirit expressed through the souls of women in every race and creed. There is a strength within us that is to be admired and honored. We will need to rely on this spirit of strength and resilience to take us from where we are to where we want to be.

It is my aim that all women regardless of age, race, creed, color, or socio-economic status take the message in this book and apply it to their lives. While women have come a long way, our value is not always clearly seen or communicated. It is time for all women to stand up and be counted among the world's leaders in every field of human endeavor.

You, my sister, are great. You are an awesome and peculiar piece of craftsmanship. Accept your greatness, except your role, open up your hearts, but stand your ground. Make your stake in the land where you stand and claim everything you desire.

As you read through the chapters in this book, I want you to imagine your life as a secret garden. In this secret garden no one knows the seeds you have decided to plant until they have fully grown. You alone decide which seeds to plant, and how to nurture those seeds. You have to keep the seeds watered and nourished so that they will grow healthy and strong. Just like a garden, in life, you have to plan for your future. You have to know what steps you will need to take to help you achieve your goals and grow your dreams. After mapping out what steps you want to take in your life, you then have to execute and manage your plan, as you would your garden.

In the management of your life plan, you have to prevent outside forces from planting "bad seeds". Bad seeds are low self-image, feelings of inadequacies, uncontrollable rage and desires—all of which manifest themselves in the form of unplanned pregnancies, STD's, drug abuse, unhealthy relationships and other distractions that cause lower than desired academic, personal or professional performance. Your secret garden is at the core of who you are in life. Protect it at all costs. Do not allow people to run or trample over your garden. Do not allow people to turn your beautiful garden into their personal garbage dump. Be mindful that there will always be people who want to destroy your garden. There will always be weeds lurking to grow amongst your garden to steal the nourishment you provide your garden. Weed negative influences out of your secret garden of life. They can and will ruin you.

If you are not attentive to your garden on a daily basis, you will not know how it is progressing. You will not notice where weeds (bad seeds) have been sown; until they grow out of control. Just as in life, things may become so unmanageable that the thoughts of giving up manifest through an attitude of complacency and apathy.

In life you have to monitor your actions daily to make sure that you are executing your vision and applying due diligence to protect it from internal and external forces that could destroy it.

I repeat–your life is your garden. What is the state of your garden now? Is it full of beautiful flowers or is it overgrown with weeds? Is your soil full of small little pebbles, rocks, candy wrappers, and other garbage that simply do not belong there? Whether you are throwing garbage in your own garden or allowing others to do so— understand it is time to do some spring cleaning. If your life is not where you want it to be, the time is now to determine what you want your life to be.

For the purposes of this book, let us imagine that we are starting over with a new garden; one that never existed before. First, we have to start by preparing our hearts for change. We have to believe that we are worthy to have a beautiful garden. We have to value our garden to the point where only the best and most beautiful flowers are able to grow there. When something is infertile, it does not have the capability of producing ANYTHING. We have to prepare the soil of our hearts to grow the plans which we desire and our destiny commands.

To prepare our hearts we have to get rid of the rocks of resentment, disappointment, hurt and pain. We must get rid of the stones of anger, jealously, rage, envy and deceit. We have to get rid of the pebbles of fear, low self-esteem, low self-worth, doubt, unbelief, anxiety and worry. We must get rid of the garbage which manifests itself in the form of lack of control, lack of discipline and low-level thinking. Replacing such garbage with love, peace, patience, kindness and temperance will help change the circumstances in your life. When and only when our hearts are cleansed of the impurities that prevent growth can we begin our journey to become the woman of our dreams.

An exercise that I do to keep my heart clean is to write down in three columns the following headlines: 1) The person who offended me; 2) What the offense was, and 3) How that offense made me feel.

I then begin to write down every minor and major offense. I then go through the list and let God know that I forgive this person, for doing this thing and making me feel this way. If you do this exercise, you will find that the third column (how the offenses made you feel) will probably be the same, repeating over and over again, just showing up with different people and situations. Why? Very simple ladies, it is what's written on the tablets of our hearts that will be manifested. For these reasons, it is most critical that we cleanse our hearts from any and everything that is not life and love.

Now that we have a clean garden full of rich, fertile soil, let's begin to plant the seeds of our future. Prepare the soil of your heart to receive these seeds of purpose, character, and destiny. Remember, protecting, nourishing, and nurturing your garden to maturity is your responsibility!

CHAPTER ONE

What's My Name?

"Tune your ears to me; set your heart on a life of understanding. That's right–if you make gaining insight your priority, and don't take 'no' for an answer, searching for it like an adventurer on a treasure hunt, before you know it, what you seek will be yours."[8]

Whether it's academic knowledge or common sense, knowledge is Queen. When one knows better it is expected that he or she will make better decisions. There is a direct correlation between the knowledge one attains and their income and quality of life. Your new goal is to seek as much knowledge as possible. It will be critical in taking you from where you are to where you want to be.

"I am freely given to those who ask–plainspoken in the form of Knowledge and Understanding. I am a rich mine of common sense for those who live well, a personal bodyguard to the candid and sincere. I will be your close friend, and my brother Knowledge is your pleasant companion. Good Sense will scout ahead for danger, and Insight will keep an eye out for you. They'll keep you from making wrong turns or following the bad directions of those who are lost themselves and can't tell a trail from a tumbleweed. These losers make a game of evil and throw parties to celebrate perversity, traveling paths that go nowhere, wandering in a maze of detours and dead ends."[9]

8 Proverbs 2:1-4. The Holy Bible (Message).
9 Proverbs 2:10-15. The Holy Bible (Message).

My sisters, do you know my name? For I will tell you to not follow the lost down doomed paths. Don't become one of those who can't tell the difference between a trail and a tumbleweed. They live for the dead ends that wait on the dark roads they travel. This is not for us. Our lives will be rich and filled with prosperity and love for ourselves and our family. What we know and understand will manifest itself in the way we live.

"Never walk away from me, for I will literally guard your life. Love me and I will keep my eyes on you. Above all and before all, seek me! Throw your arms around me–believe and trust in me, you won't regret it. Never let me go–I'll make your life glorious. I'll garland your life with grace, and ornament your days with beauty."[10] Take my advice; it will add years to your life.

It is time for an about face! The time has come to seek knowledge and apply what we know. When you know better, it makes no sense to make the same mistakes over and over again. You can no longer blame others for the bad choices you make. About face! Attaining knowledge can and will drive you to live a better and more prosperous life. Without knowledge and the understanding, it

10 Proverbs 4:6-9. The Holy Bible.

brings–you are doomed to struggle and make poor decisions that destroy the garden of your life. Not attempting to acquire as much knowledge as possible is practically suicide.

Remember to call me by my name as you go about your daily activities. *"When you find me, you find life and receive favor from the Lord. But if you wrong me, you damage your very soul; when you reject me, know that you are flirting with death."*[11]

"Beloved, take to heart what I'm telling you; collect my counsel and guard them with your life."[12]

There are principles, patterns, and laws that govern life and whether or not you choose to believe that they are relevant to your life does not make you exempt from their rewards and consequences. The old saying that you reap what you sow has passed the test of time because it was just as true 2,000 years ago as it is today. Some call it reciprocity, some call it karma, but whatever you call it, what you do, say, and think will dictate what you get out of life.

11 Proverbs 8:35-36. The Holy Bible.
12 Proverbs 2:1. The Holy Bible.

If we really understood this, we would not do half of the things we do. Many of the behaviors that we invest our time and energy into bring us absolutely negative results that cost us immeasurably. To move from where we are to the women we want to be, we have to do the things that will sow the seeds of peace, prosperity, and limitless growth.

What's My Name? They Call Me Lady Wisdom!
I Lady Wisdom am freely given to those who ask.

Remember, Independent Women use Wisdom!

CHAPTER TWO
All of the Lights

I want you to picture yourself walking blindfolded through a busy street toward your destination. How far do you think you will get without bumping into something or getting seriously injured? How scared would you feel not knowing what is in front of you? The truth of the matter is that without sight you will not get far without injuring yourself. Light allows you to clearly see the paths that you are taking so that you can see those things that would otherwise cause you to stumble. Where there is light, there are fewer mistakes, less bumps and bruises. Not only is your immediate pathway clearer, you are also able to see farther down the road.

Turning on your lights is about your search for knowledge—the lamp unto your path. When turned on, this light will help guide your mind, body, and soul in the direction of truth. This light will help you become a better woman; a real woman. Do you have all of your lights on?

The light helps you physically as it guides you to present your body as a living sacrifice, one that is holy and acceptable to the Lord. It will guide you to eat right, exercise, and treat your body as the temple and dwelling place of God. I think we can all agree that our situations could use a touch from God. Sometimes, women, we treat our bodies

7

in the most profane manner. I cannot stress enough–every time we have unprotected sex or use drugs, we are absolutely destroying the most precious thing we have. Remember, our body is a temple, not a garbage dump. Keep trash out! We must protect our body as it is the only one, we will ever have.

The longer you wait for sex, the better. Sex involves a great deal of risk and responsibility–risks and responsibilities that you do not need or want. When sex goes bad, it goes really bad. Ask anybody who has gotten pregnant before they were ready or contracted a sexually transmitted disease. They wish they could turn back the hands of time, but those choices can never be corrected.

Just like hindsight, foresight is 20/20. Now that you know better, plan to do what's right for your body.

The light helps you mentally as it gives you the ability to think, plan, and take on the mind of purpose. It guides you to make decisions that serve your long-term needs and goals. It prevents you from doing things that appear to be right for right now or popular right now, but that you will regret to your core later. The light brings clarity of vision, singleness of eye and the focus of an eagle. In other words it helps to eliminate distractions and helps you overcome setbacks.

The light helps you become strong emotionally. It gives you the ability to guard and guide your heart because it affects everything that you do. It allows you to bring your emotions under your control; otherwise they will absolutely lead you in the wrong direction. Whether it's vain love, lust, anger, wrath, vengeance, or jealously, the light will act as a traffic light which shows us when to stop, go, or slow down. Our emotions often give us a green light to do things that are not in our best interest. Allowing better judgment to guide you empowers you to say "no" to things that you know will hurt you in the long run. You must not be afraid to let better judgment be your guide.

The light gives liberty to your spirit. Understand that we are spirit first; we possess a soul and live in a body. You are not a human being trying to become spiritual; but you are a spiritual being having a human experience. Shifting your mind-set to think like this may be difficult but very necessary.

There is no need to do things which give an outward appearance of pleasing God for it is impossible to please God without faith. Your belief that HE IS is enough to please him. Understanding that faith without works is dead, requires putting action to what it is you say you believe.

The light will guide your spirit into deeper levels of love which are evident in how you treat others and yourself. It calls you to a higher standard and quality of life. The light will help you to identify and expose those who mean you harm and or danger. It will illuminate the eyes of your understanding to keep those people away that plan to ruin the life that you plan for yourself.

Understand that some people are afraid to succeed. These people will seek to tear you down at every opportunity. When you come in contact with a person who desires to be a part of your life, ask yourself if this person will add to your life, subtract from your life, bring multiplication to your life or bring division. It should not take years to answer this question.

As you can clearly see, having all of the lights on is a critical component to you becoming a real woman. Thankfully this light does not require you to open your physical eyes. This light is provided for us through our faith in God. 2 Corinthians 5:7 says, "We walk by faith, and not by sight." Your faith in God will keep you on the right path, and bring out the absolute best in you; so much so that it will become contagious to everyone you come in contact with.

When you have all of these lights, you cannot go wrong. Becoming the woman, you want to be will require you to have all of your lights on.

It is critical that you start preparing your heart as soon as possible to commit to your life's purpose. Committing to a life of purpose is not easy. Don't expect it to be. It will have its ups and downs, but it takes special people to become all that they can be. Many fall because they are afraid to let their lights shine because it offends those who live in the dark, or makes them different from others who choose not to live life with purpose. My sisters, I beg you to let your light shine before men so that they may see your good deeds!

In the event you are approached by a guy, you should stop, look and listen! Look for signs that he has his lights on. Don't just look at his physical appearance; although you should be able to see that he cares about his body and outward appearance. He should be clean and well-kept. Most importantly, however, try to analyze where his mind is, and what he wants from you. If you know that he is only trying to get to know you to add you to the list of women he has conquered, he is not the man for you. If he is committed to negativity or criminal behavior, he is not for you. If he does not have any dreams, goals, and aspirations that he is working toward, he is not for you. If his faith is not totally, fully planted in God, he is most certainly not for you.

Stop right where you are and find a quiet place. If there is noise where you are, simply remove yourself and go to a quiet place for the next ten minutes. I need for you to do some soul searching; but before you do that, I need you to clear your head completely. You must be thinking about nothing else but the words coming off of this page.

Look, observe, take notice and pay attention to the trends that are happening within your community. Take notice of the prison rates amongst African American males and females. Take notice of the dropout rates. Take notice of the number of children born out of wedlock into single parent homes. Take notice of how drugs have ravaged communities across the nation. Take notice of how a lack of education causes many single mothers to become permanently dependent on the welfare system. Take notice to the number of women who have contracted HIV. Take notice to the acts of violence and blatant injustices. These things are troubling and awaiting a solution.

These ills in society are why I bring you this book. We must stand up and make a difference in society. It starts with us as individuals. We must do everything we can to prevent having children out of wedlock. We must do everything we can to protect ourselves from sexually transmitted diseases. We must do everything we can to be as prosperous and self-sufficient as possible. We must be able to provide for ourselves and our families so that they do not grow to contribute to crime and further destruction of our communities. It is time that we become better women that care and put into action solutions to the critical needs of our communities.

Now look at the media and entertainment industry. Often you see degrading images of women as sex symbols. This is not all bad in the sense that women are beautiful, and being beautiful is a part of our femininity. Sometimes it's appropriate to show your curves; however, it is critical to know when it is not appropriate to do so. I would suggest that in most situations you dress to draw attention to parts of you other than your butt, thighs, and breasts. If you focus on showing your curves, most people won't attempt to see past that. Remember, the best parts of you, your mind, heart and character, are on the inside. Developing these elements to the degree that they make you radiant requires hard work. Only women who lack inner beauty compensate for it with an explicit dress code. To think that all you are worth is a nice butt and a smile is dangerous. Bad things are sure to come when you attract people who are only interested in your body. You had better make sure that you have your mind, heart, *and* spirit intact. You had better understand that the more flesh you show, and the more of your private parts you show, the more the value of your stock goes down. Be more than pretty, sexy, or cute. Be smart and intelligent. Demand respect for more than just your body, or you will, in essence, demand that people respect you for less than what you are. LADIES, YOUR BEST ASSET IS NOT YOUR BUTT!

As women, we simply want others to love us as deeply as we love. Because many of us grow up not truly loving and respecting ourselves we begin to believe that receiving true love and respect is a fairy tale. Eventually we begin to accept degrading ourselves for the benefit and pleasure of others who degrade us. We must understand that we do not need the validation of others to make us feel beautiful or loved. True love starts from within. When you truly love yourself, you will not degrade yourself in any way, shape, form, or fashion; nor will you accept being degraded by anyone else. The time is now to love ourselves first. Only after we love ourselves will we be able to wisely identify who truly loves us.

In many cases, young ladies give in to having sex before it is time to avoid the pain of rejection and abandonment by the man they are attracted to. Ladies... lust has an appetite that will never be satisfied. The man who does not truly care about you will lay down with you and any woman that he can to satisfy the lust that drives him. He does not have his mind, body, and soul in order and can only be a danger to you. If you lay down with a man who does not truly care about you or value the essence of who you are, you might as well lay down with a filthy pig. Daughter, you are placing your precious jewels before swine only to have them trampled on. Afterwards you will be left feeling alone, dirty and ashamed; rejected, misused and still searching to be loved.

Do not cast your pearls before swine; never devalue yourself for the sake of a dirty pig. Saving yourself will only increase the value of your stock, and increase your self-worth. Remember self-esteem is love for yourself! No one can give it to you, nor can anyone take it away.

The fact of the matter is that men and women abuse sex. It is often used recreationally to help us numb pains that we experience and hold inside of us. It leads people to have sex recklessly and produce children that they cannot afford and eventually regret having. Because the sex was recreational and not between two people in a lifelong commitment of marriage, circumstances are made much worse for everybody involved–the mother, the father, and the child. Ladies, this is not the way. Avoid unplanned pregnancy at all cost! Let me repeat that. Avoid unplanned pregnancy at all cost!!! Just as abortion is not a contraceptive, getting pregnant is no accident. Getting pregnant is no accident. When all of your lights are on, and your mind, heart, and soul are intact, you will make the decision to abstain from sex altogether or certainly use protection every time you have sex.

If you have yet to have a child, you are in a great place to plan and execute your plan. If you have had a child or more out of wedlock or have been abusing sex, now is the time that you are honest with yourself and realize where you made the decision to struggle. Now make a declaration that struggle will not be a lifestyle but a temporary condition in your life. Go back to that place in your mind and understand what lead you to make the mistakes you made and prepare for the next chapter in the book of your life.

No matter where you are in life, the book of your life is an on-going work. We must work on each page one day at a time. Never forget the woman you are trying to become, and make sure that everything you do on a daily basis is proof positive of the direction you are headed.

This daily walk is the hardest part of the process of growth and development. Knowledge alone is fruitless. When you can apply what you know, that is when you begin to show wisdom. My goal is to not only encourage you to attain knowledge, but to also show you how to apply what you know in order for you to grow. No matter where you are, know that you can always be better.

Remember, Independent Women use Wisdom
and Let their Light Shine!

CHAPTER THREE
The Empire State of Mind

No matter where you are or where you have been, you can become anything you want to be. Your attitude about what you want to be and the energy you apply to get there is directly connected to whether or not you will reach your goals. You must possess a conviction strong enough to change the course of your life through your actions and attitude.

As a native New Yorker, I entitled this chapter "The Empire State of Mind" because that is where you need to be mentally to accomplish your dreams. New York is filled with limitless potential for prosperity, just as it is filled with limitless obstacles and distractions waiting to snare you in their traps. Just like life, New York is filled with danger and opportunity. It is often said that if you can make it in New York you can make it anywhere in the world. Well, my sisters, I want you to assume the mentality that you can and will make it anywhere. We are all vulnerable to traps and obstacles, but we must never accept defeat. You must have the internal heart and guts to thrive. It starts mentally, but it takes much more than that. It takes the ability to be fearless! No matter where you are in the world, understand that the race is not given to the swift, but to the one that endures to the end. This road to success is not for the faint of heart! I repeat... this road to pursuing your destiny and call of God on your life is not for the faint of heart, or in other words, weak hearted. It is not about the blows you give, but the ones you are able to take and keep on standing. Let's exercise our mind, heart, and spirit to be ready, to thrive and take us from where we are to where we want to be.

You may or may not think much of who you are, why you are here, or for what purpose on earth you were created, but I promise you, you are here on this earth for a reason. A significant assignment and a great problem await your solution. It's up to you to stand up and fulfill your destiny. No one will do it for you.

Ladies, understand that your attitude is nothing more than how you choose to view circumstances and situations. These views are shaped by a culmination of experiences; lessons learned and information you have acquired. The operative word is choose. Your attitude is a choice! It will determine how you approach matters and it is your approach that will determine success or failure. Let me help you establish or re-define a belief and value system that will stand up to everything that may be holding you back internally and externally. It is these ten (10) foundational principles that helped me to think differently about myself and my situation.

21

These principles helped me to establish my empire state of mind attitude and a new outlook on life.

Principle #1: I Am Not My Circumstances

Your circumstances are temporary realities that can absolutely be changed. Before you embark on your journey of self-transformation, I encourage you to repeat a simple prayer daily:

> *Father, you said that I am the head and not the tail, above and not beneath, a lender and not a borrower, wealth and riches are in my house, everything my hand touches prospers and today I make a conscious decision to believe that I am everything you say that I am!*

Your circumstances are training courses which will prepare you to progress to the next stage in your life if you can overcome the obstacles and evade the traps that will be set for you at each stage. It will take wisdom, a strong heart, a bold spirit and mental toughness to face them head on. Circumstances change in the direction in which you change them. While you are in the process of changing your situation understand there will be times when you have done everything in your power and things still may not work out; be still and give thanks! There will be times when you will do absolutely nothing, and the opportunity of a lifetime presents itself... run through the open door and give thanks!

Principle #2: My Life is Not a Mistake

You must know that before the foundation of the world, God had a plan for your life. The blessing of life is not only a blessing and a privilege, it also comes with a responsibility–to find your purpose and fulfill it here on earth. My parents may not have intentionally planned on my arrival; life comes from God. If I could do and accomplish what you were created to do, then there would be no reason for you being here. Although man makes many mistakes; God makes no mistakes!

Principle #3: No Matter How Good or Bad My Actions, God Loves Me No More or Less

This was probably the most important revelation that I received. God loves us no matter how much we mess up. "For who shall separate us from the love of God? Shall trouble or hardship or persecution or famine or nakedness or danger or sword?"[13] No, in all these things we are more than conquerors through Him who loves us. Though

---

13 Proverbs 2:10-15. The Holy Bible.

you will never be perfect, serving your purpose is the perfect show of love and honor to God—because we do this through faith and obedience. It is God's crazy, mad love for us that draws us closer to Him to the point where we want to change our ways. Man will have you bound up with religious do's and don'ts, wearing dresses every day, no make-up, earrings, etc. while trying to do something outwardly to be holy or righteous. Nothing we do will ever make us holy or righteous outside of receiving Him; we are capable, adequate and sufficient because He lives in hopes to one day live within us.

Principle #4: Live to Serve

Can one say he or she loves God and not love his fellow man?[14] People profess their love for God, yet they act in ways that are not love toward their fellowman and communities.

I discovered that my purpose was to serve and help others even though I still needed help myself. I was a once struggling single welfare mother with four children, working and in school full time struggling to make ends meet and penalized for every dollar I made. I was determined to not be like those who say with their mouths they believe, but in their hearts don't believe.

I John 4:20

24

I got off my butt and made it my business to serve others in every capacity I could. In turn, my life was changed through the power of serving others. My life, which at one time looked like a pile of ashes, was exchanged over time for beauty, grace and distinction. Your love for God will always be shown by how you treat others.

Principle #5: Don't be Afraid of Men and their Faces

Stand up and be counted! Men look at the outward appearance, but God looks at the heart. Don't let the sexism, racism, bigotry, and hatred that others spew upon you to affect how you feel about yourself and the vigor in which you approach living the life you want to live. Free yourself from this mental hell. It was not until I found out who I was that I became strong in the sense that I could look any man or woman in the eye and express myself freely with confidence. Regardless of how you look or what you currently have to offer, understand that you are special. God made every man and woman equally special in their own way. Respect the special uniqueness of others, and always respect and love your own unique characteristics.

Principle #6: I Will Have to Give An Account of My Time and Talents

This was hard to handle the first time I heard that there will be a day where we will have to give an account of how we used our time and talents. Gifts and talents are given to every man along with a measure of faith. It is BAD, BAD like Michael Jackson BAD when we bury our talents in the ground. I did whatever was necessary to develop my talents. Whatever your talents are, sharpen and use them to serve mankind and not yourself. I started with the one gift that I noticed. It was my ability to write and express myself. I began with poetry as I had dreams of being the next Maya Angelou and having my writings all over the world. I started a small business making greeting cards encouraging others. Every experience that I had using my talents opened more doors for me. Using your special talents will do the same for you.

Principle #7: Your Gifts Makes Room for You

When I read that my gift will make room for me, the only concern I had was to develop that gift to the point where it would bring me into the presence of great men and women. Just as using my gifts did for me, using your gifts will grant you access to important people, places and things. Who knew that one day the gift of writing would lead me to write books, public policies and one day legislation?

In developing my gift, I was taught that the thing that really gets you upset, and I mean very upset is the one thing that you were created to change. We all have different temperaments and tolerance levels and the thing that takes you from zero to eighty in 3.3 seconds is an indicator of what you will not tolerate; hence the thing that you will influence and change. Remember, what you are willing to tolerate, you are not willing to change.

There are seven mountains/pillars in our society. They are: 1) Government, 2) Business, 3) Arts and Entertainment, 4) Media, 5) Education, 6) Family, and 7) Church. Your gifts will be used in one of these mountains.

Keep in mind that your gifts are not for you. They were given to you to serve others. I had to stay focused on using my gifts in this capacity. I had no time to waste on issues and people that would only block my success. Using your gifts will help you meet new people who can help you along your journey to bigger and better things. Remember patience is a virtue—an admirable quality that takes time to develop; so, let patience have her perfect work!

Principle #8: God's Will is Not Automatic; It Takes the Cooperation of Man

If you give it to God, everything will be fine. Don't worry about it; God is going to do it. Well, the more I learned about life the more I learned that there was something missing in this message. When God blesses you with talents and abilities, it is up to you to employ them within the geographical jurisdiction you have been assigned. Understand that the gifts of God are without repentance. This means that although God has given these gifts to you, he never violates our freedom to choose how we use those gifts. If we decided to serve ourselves in vanity, he will never regret ever giving the gift to us. We are not puppets with strings attached to us. When we acknowledge God in all our ways, He will give us the plan and give light to our understanding as to how we use our gift; it is up to us to translate and implement this divine inspiration into a manifested reality. This is when you begin to take the learning of your mind to the place where the passion of your heart meets the talents of your hands; it is in this place where you will make a difference.

I want you to understand that God will never violate your freedom to choose. Your next blessing will come from the hands of a human being. The quicker you cooperate with God's Will, the better off WE will all be.

Principle #9: A Wise Person Knows That They Know Nothing At All
People are strange and peculiar; each on a unique journey to finding out truth. There is but one definition for truth. Truth needs no

defense for it is an absolute, which means nothing can be added to it and nothing taken away from it. It stands all by itself regardless of who chooses to believe.

Many of us would love to boast upon the knowledge we have acquired and revelations we have received, however, one person's understanding or perspective is pale when it is compared to the whole truth. There is a wealth of knowledge to attain that will empower you to achieve your goals in life and serve others if you pursue it. Seek to learn something new every day. The natural mind can only conceive what it has been exposed to, but there is so much more to learn. Therefore, go through life with the mindset that you are here to learn everything you can about whom you are and the arena that you have been assigned to. In other words master your craft! Never be comfortable with what you know. Always seek to learn more. But understand that no matter how much you learn; know that you know nothing at all.

Principle #10: Guard your Heart for it Affects Everything You Do

Ladies, if I told you what I had to endure to get to this place surely you would not believe me. After I realized the power of negative circumstances and situations to steal my dreams, I understood that I had to make sure that I controlled them and not the other way around. I was determined to make it to the finish line and in doing that I had to make sure that my emotions were kept in proper perspective.

I made a decision that my garden would be made of the most beautiful examples of God's creations. I would never let hate, anger and unhappiness darken the beauty in my garden. Every day I confessed positive things in my life, and asked God to help me be able to protect my heart and my dreams from negativity. I surrendered my heart to God and let Him have every secret, every deceiving thought, every desire and every longing. My circumstances and situations now belonged to Him and you can call it faith or trust, but I knew I would be safe and successful.

You have heard the phrase "Welfare Mentality" used when describing people who refuse to think beyond their circumstances. This is the mentality you do not want to adopt. Individuals with this mind state are always looking to take and get over, always looking to receive, they believe someone owes them something and therefore refuse to work for what they want. This mental state will cripple you; it will stifle your vision and dreams from becoming a reality and it will most certainly keep you poor and in need of public assistance.

The principles above have helped me create the very necessary empire state of mind that I have today. Many people never get to live and profit from their gifts. Most of us get stuck and settle for less because it is easier to do. It is easier to give way to excuses and quit. It is easier to give into circumstances and payback others who have wronged you. Vengeance does not belong to you; it belongs to God!

The empire state of mind is bigger than your circumstances; it is bigger than your financial status and the limits you allow others to set on you. There is no vision that is too big or no gift that is too small for you to create the life you dream about.

Remember, Independent Women use Wisdom,

Let their Light Shine and Take on the Empire State of Mind!

CHAPTER FOUR
Heartless

In writing the brother version of this book, *Get Your Hands Out of My Pocket: The Hands-On Guide to Avoiding the Child Support System*, the one theme that was prevalent throughout the sixty something men that participated in the book review was the cruel nature of a scorned woman. Brothers could not understand how women could be so cold and heartless in getting revenge for hurt feelings. I would often find myself laughing inside as I noticed the intensity of their perplexity. So, I thought without a doubt the heart of the woman had to be discussed.

As a woman thinks in her heart, so is she. The heart has over forty-thousand nerve cells which allow it to function and operate like a brain. The heart, when focused on positive emotions such as appreciation, compassion, care and love radiates the largest electro-magnetic field produced in the body. This electro-magnetic field can produce a force that is felt some three to twenty feet away–thus having the capacity to affect everything within its circumference. It is not so much the thoughts in the brain in our heads, but the brain in our hearts that has the power to transform the circumstances in our life. The heart will typically beat out a different message from the brain which causes the two to conflict. The heart is more powerful than the brain and getting the two on the same page is a constant challenge.

When the two are on one accord; communication, relationships, and productivity improve.

In my prayer time one morning, I checked in and asked God to search my heart and cleanse it from any impure thing. Immediately the face of my father came up and I said to God, reveal to me what is there. I asked God what it was that I was holding on to. He showed me that it was a deep-rooted feeling of resentment. I asked myself why I resented my father... I thought I had gotten over that a long time ago. Then God began to show me what my father should have done. I saw the face of my father telling me that I was beautiful, adequate and more than enough; that I was perfect the way that I was and any man would die to be a part of my life. As I began to feel the pain and emptiness of what it felt like to never have heard those words, I began to cry like a baby. God showed me that it was because I had never heard those words that I sought for the validation of my beauty through other men, especially older men. Had I been given that confirmation and assurance by my father there is no way I would have chosen half the men I had relationships with.

That thought was a huge eye opener for me in that many of my mistakes were caused by unconscious needs and feelings that

I harbored deep inside. The truth of the matter is that we make decisions from a knowledge base stored within us. This knowledge base of past hurts and pains guide our thoughts and decisions. Sometimes they prevent us from thinking and behaving rationally. Sometimes they drive us to seek love from abusive relationships and sometimes take our anger out on the people that genuinely love us.

It is critical that we check in with our heart at all times. We have to take an inventory of our hearts intentions and motivations. When we become acquainted with our heart–we are better able to articulate exactly what it is we are feeling. We do this by first keeping negative emotions far from us. When we are faced with feelings like anger, envy, hate, or jealousy we have to immediately check and evaluate those feelings.

I will be the first to tell you that there were times when I could not celebrate the victories and triumphs of others. I used to smile and say things like, "oh that sounds great," when in my heart I was jealous that it was not me receiving that blessing or benefiting from that opportunity. One day I decided that I would celebrate with others because I would want others to celebrate with me. Did it take some practice? Absolutely! Do I now bask in the victories of others with a caring and happy heart? Yes, I do. Why? Because I have made great accomplishments myself and look forward to the same in others; so if you find yourself hating inwardly, simply change the activities in your life and do things that others would want to applaud and celebrate.

Heartless is not just about flowing in a mean and evil spirit day in and day out. It is about being void of love, purpose and meaningful direction in your life. Being heartless is ignoring the most powerful weapon you have. You will lose the fight if and when you battle with NO HEART! Heart is about having courage and being bold in the face of adversity. It is about being mature in the midst of complex emotions and being peaceful in the midst of conflict. It is about loving those who hate and spitefully use you. Having heart is TO LOVE NO MATTER WHAT!

Training the heart to endure and not faint is the first step to avoid becoming heartless. Emotions flow from the heart; therefore, it is vital that we do not let our emotions get in the way of constructive communication. We must not let our emotions prevent us from communicating our message clearly with others or prevent us from listening to what others have to say. The heart is like Grand Central Station. For those who have never been to Grand Central Station; it is the largest train station in the world and it is located in Manhattan, New York. Some few thousand commuters come through Grand Central Station on a daily basis; similar to our heart which interprets thousands of emotions, ideas and intentions on a daily basis.

Until your heart has had time to develop and mature, it is recommended that you create what I call a "safe place". The safe place is a place in your heart where there is no judgment of others, NO prejudices, stereotypes or biases. It is a place where you don't seek to offend or be defensive. Whenever you are dealing with a stressful and or hurtful situation, place your heart in the safe place. Imagine that this safe place is a refuge for your heart. There can only be thoughts, feelings and emotions of love, appreciation, care, and compassion that bring you peace and positivity. Communicating from this safe place demonstrates to others that your intentions are friendly yet honest, and your ability to be transparent does not make you vulnerable. Communicating from the safe place brings positive results and builds healthy relationships.

Our negative reactions to hurt feelings only make us feel better temporarily. When we allow the emotions in our heart to get the best of us, they normally cause us to make poor decisions that lead to undesirable consequences that destroy relationships or take time and money to repair. When we are hurt we often respond with vengeful, vindictive behaviors from slashing tires to suing for child support just because it causes an inconvenience to others. We must be able to communicate and react above and beyond our feelings to bring about the positive results that we intentionally want to create.

You must be proactive in addressing situations that are unfair or make you feel uncomfortable. If there is something that makes you angry or feel bad, it is critical that you address it as soon as you notice it and take every measure to prevent it from happening again. There is no need in slashing your boyfriend's tires because you caught him cheating. If he is a cheater, the best thing to do is leave him. Infidelity can be a form of abuse and abuse leads to more and more abuse.

That is precisely the reason why you must increase your emotional intelligence (EQ). Our EQ is simply the ability to recognize, evaluate, and command mastery of our emotions and those of others. This takes discipline and a very mature heart. My definition of EQ is when the heart and mind flow on the same accord, whereas they both strengthen one another to stay the course; neither one will allow the other to become distracted—thus producing oneness of strength and high actionable intelligence.

Increasing your EQ will help you to avoid becoming the abuse you experience. Once you become abusive in response to the pain that you feel inside, you create a cycle of dysfunction that grows like a cancer. This abuse eats away at your soul and makes you and everyone else around you suffer. Your inability to emotionally mature manifests itself in the form of repeated illogical and irrational behavior that causes you to fail personally and professionally.

Do not repay anyone evil for evil. Be careful to do what is right in the eyes of everyone[15]. In other words, rise above the drama. Be slow to anger. Remember that when you dig a ditch for others you also dig a ditch for yourself. As you speak death unto others, you too will eat the fruit of that destruction. As you attempt to hold that person in the ditch, you are trapped in the same ditch with them. This is clearly not the answer to freeing ourselves from pain or finding the love and sustenance we need to win the race.

You must become the love that you want to receive in your life. Life has a funny way of bringing you what you truly want and deserve. When you become the woman of your dreams you don't need to respond to negativity. Real women don't respond to

14 Romans 12:17. The Holy Bible

negative situations in negative ways. We rise above the fray. In order to accomplish this, you must rid yourself of negative people. Bad company corrupts good character.[16] When you encounter hurtful situations you must: 1. identify what hurts you, 2. seek to prevent it from happening again, 3. forgive and 4. move on with your life focusing on constant personal and professional progress.

Heartless people are hurt people who don't know a better way than to hurt other people. They are stuck in a cycle of pain. Their paradigm of what defines life is simply different from people who seek happiness and maturity. When you become love, you will attract people and circumstances that love in the same manner. When you allow hurt, vengeance, and neediness to dictate your behavior–you attract more and more of the same. Instead of being vindictive; your motivation is to start to shed people and circumstances that harm you altogether and remain strong and loving in the face of hurtful situations.

In the process of gaining heart and mastering your emotions, don't forget to take an inventory of the relationships that you are involved in. Determine whether or not they are relationships that

15 I Corinthians 15:33

help you or hurt you. Some of us turn to lust and the servitude of abusive men to validate our beauty or fill voids in our lives. My sisters, as you begin to gain strength in your heart, do whatever you must to guard your heart from those who don't deserve access. Denying access to some may look like being alone during certain times of your life. Many women are afraid of being by themselves and so they deal with the barbaric and unseemly behaviors of others to avoid being lonely. When you begin to love who you are and who you are becoming—you will eventually enjoy your own company. Anything should be better than being in the presence of those who merely tolerate you. Begin to condition yourself to only be in the presence of those who celebrate you.

Remember, when one does not understand the purpose of a thing, abuse is inevitable. How can we value anything that we do not understand? Understanding the heart and all its strengths and weaknesses will help you accomplish the unthinkable. There are limitless things you are capable of doing and the first will start with you loving yourself. After all, if we don't love ourselves, how can we expect others to do so? Your life is worth more than that. You are worthy of love. This you must be rock solid on.

Understand, lust is insatiable, in other words, it has an appetite that can never be satisfied. Be careful that you are not led away by your own lustful desires. These activities will destroy and corrupt the heart. The eyes are never satisfied, and they will always pursue bigger and better if you let them. Whenever you are controlled by lust or vice, you submit your will to the failure that vice will certainly bring you. For the one who sows to her own flesh will from the flesh reap corruption, but the one who sows to the Spirit will from the Spirit reap eternal life[17]. The spirit of God flows in love, joy, peace, kindness, patience, goodness and self-control–all of which are central to having a strong heart.

Seek God's purpose for your life and make that pursuit your daily business. The void in your life that you may feel is the absence of purpose. When you don't understand the purpose in which you were created, you will abuse your time, talent and treasure. An example of what abusing your time looks like is simply having too much of it. Too much time on your hands to do nothing leads to an idle and unproductive life. When we are idle and unproductive, we will let anything come in to occupy and take space just to pass the time. Things such as recreational sex, drug and alcohol abuse are

Galatians 6:8. The Holy Bible

activities that feed more poor decision making. Devote yourself to finding your purpose and serve it with all your heart.

I Corinthians 13: 4-7 changed my perspective on what love is. I want to share with you the real meaning of love. "Love is patient, love is kind. It does not envy, it does not boast, it is not proud. It does not dishonor others, it is not self-seeking, it is not easily angered, and it keeps no record of wrongs. Love does not delight in evil but rejoices with the truth. It always protects, always trusts, always hopes, and always perseveres[18]." These verses tell us what love is, ladies. If the love you have doesn't meet these standards, then it is not love at all. Redefine love for yourselves. That is what being R.E.A.L is all about– Redefining Everything About Life and Love. Don't just demand the love you deserve; be the love you deserve. By setting a high standard for the love you desire and the love that you live by, only true love will find you.

18 I Corinthians 13:4-7. The Holy Bible.

Remember, Independent Women use Wisdom,

Let their Light Shine,

Take on the Empire State of Mind

and Have Heart!

CHAPTER FIVE
Avoid the Welfare Trap

Let's be clear, social assistance the government provides in terms of affordable housing and food and nutrition benefits are very real and vital for many struggling to survive. These resources are without a doubt especially necessary for many single mothers to provide a stable and healthy environment for their children.

However, taking on these resources comes at a price. There is a point where government support becomes so comfortable that it becomes a trap that robs you of the motivation to gain wealth and find financial independence.

The word "support" means "to bear-up and hold upright". The word "trapped" means the total opposite. Trapped means "to be held tightly by something and cannot move or be freed."

While the welfare system offers much needed support and assistance, it can easily become a trap- a life of never ending poverty and government dependency.

"Welfare-Trap" is that sunken place where one chooses to live dependent on the government for survival. While this support offers some degree of stability it requires you to commit yourself to living below the poverty line. It requires you to give up your dreams. It requires you to give up being the best you can be.

There is a distinct difference between being supported on your road to self-sufficiency (independence) and being trapped in the welfare system (dependence).

The road to self-sufficiency requires taking advantage of programs that advance education and economic opportunities that will lead to financial freedom, homeownership and greater earnings. These programs exist and are readily available to you, but you must make it a priority to take advantage of them.

The road to dependence is marked by making the least amount of money possible to maintain public assistance benefits, giving away the possibility of economic growth. The road to dependence leads you to intentionally earn the absolute minimum instead of the maximum. You shouldn't be seeking to earn the minimum! You should be working to achieve your maximum potential!

Whether you have decided to pursue your dreams or still just trying to figure out how to survive, this book is written to inspire you! To motivate you to strive for more. However, I know escaping the welfare trap is easier said than done. I know, because I am a testament of what it takes to defeat it.

For you to successfully march out of the welfare trap and onto the road to economic independence, you will need to know what to do, how to do it, and how to get help. This book is written to help provide a light on your pathway because once you make the decision to move forward towards a life of self-sufficiency and financial independence, you will begin to rapidly feel the decline in public assistance- IF you are not prepared.

Policies that regulate public assistance create a hard cap on earnings which makes the decision whether to live a life of dependency or independency more difficult. For many people living in poverty, earning more means losing much needed housing and food benefits. Small raises in earnings from working class wages can't compare to the benefits afforded by government assistance, therefore the choice between earning more or waiting around on government assistance is not much of a choice at all- it's a no brainer.

The fear of losing benefits is one of the primary reasons many people do not work to earn more. This fear is what makes many who receive various forms of public assistance stay under the radar with just enough low "reportable" wages to maintain the level of benefits necessary to maintain the basic needs of their families.

My vision for you goes well beyond waiting around for government assistance for your survival. In fact, should you choose, your future does not include fighting for survival. My vision is to help you achieve the level of prosperity you desire and are willing to work for.

I want to help you find your life's purpose, lead you to find the education and resources necessary to be successful at what you love doing, motivate you to work to earn and save more, and lastly to teach you how to build wealth and financial freedom.

The welfare system can be a trap if you do not plan to take advantage of the programs and resources it offers to help you become financially independent. Instead of allowing yourself to become permanently trapped, make a plan and execute your plan to make your current situation your launching pad.

No matter what, the one most important factor in determining your future is YOU. No one, and I mean no one, can determine whether you fail or succeed but you.

My mission is to support you along your journey to becoming the independent woman of your dreams. I can give you the blueprint, and I can provide support, but the rest is up to you.

Do you want to become the best you that you can be?

The next page is a chart with descriptive characteristics of a dependent versus independent woman. They have two different lifestyles.

Keep in mind you may very well see that you have some dependent characteristics. Don't be offended. Just know that you have work to do. Changes to make. Whatever you do, DO NOT ignore what must be done to change your life for the better.

Embrace the woman you want to become. You are already half way there...

Dependent Woman	Independent Woman
Satisfied with low level of education and professional training	Understands the importance of education and actively pursues it, for she uses the knowledge as a tool to acquire power and wealth
Does not have a desire to work to earn a living; lazy and apathetic about earning a living	Will work two jobs if necessary; Understands that working is the only way to be free from a lifestyle of "hand-outs"
No planning for the future and lives in the moment; Wants to get out of the struggle but simply is not willing to do what is required of her	Will delay instant gratification; will sacrifice short term satisfaction for long term goals; makes sure her day-to-day activities help toward achieving long term goals
Manipulates the welfare system and people through dishonesty and lies; cheats and steals to get by and is convinced she is winning when she behaves in this manner	Characterized by having good integrity; Does not depend on hustling government entitlement programs or people as a way of life;
Demonstrates anger at parent partner; disrespects the father in front of the children; holds kids as pawns in a game; won't allow children to see dad when dad asks; takes the anger out on children	She lets love and forgiveness guide her; demonstrates respect for the father of children under all circumstances; she guides him to be a better father and co-parent; She tries at all costs to maintain a positive open line of communication for the sake of the children; she pursues peace at all costs
Uses her body as a tool for ill-gotten gain; degrades herself in terms of promiscuity; wears revealing and explicit clothing	Understands her value and self-worth; respects herself and demands respect from others; she refuses to expose her body in a distasteful manner; will not be treated as a sex object

Dependent Woman	Independent Woman
Has no priorities or plans for her life and therefore; spends more time partying and having fun	Goes out socially when she needs to get away, but is conscious of where she spends her leisure time; She prefers places that are safe, clean, and reflects her image; She would not be seen in the club every weekend
Engages in unhealthy and possibly dangerous relationships	She looks for positive relationships that are mutually nourishing; stays away from relationships that are harmful
Places relationships with men before her goals, children and family	Will be single to keep peace and purpose in her life; Does not need a man nor anyone else to validate her, she lives by sound principals
Neglects her children and family priorities	Children are a top priority and their needs supersede hers, they fuel her and keep her focused
Mental health declines and is unable to maintain a clean, healthy and positive living environment	Cleanliness and order are priorities in keeping her house, mind, body, and spirit in order
Life out of control, has little to no boundaries, spends money on drugs; and will use drugs in front of her children	Will eliminate her substance abuse activities and get help to reprioritize her life; Will not jeopardize the children's health and would never expose her kids to drugs
Lacks basic life management systems and discipline; spends money foolishly neglecting her priorities (i.e. paying rent, being evicted in subsidized housing)	Spends money wisely, saves money, spends money on priorities first and luxuries last

Dependent Woman	Independent Woman
Publicly behaves loud and disrespectful; allows her emotions to get the best of her	High emotional intelligence; knows what to say and when to say it; Uses discretion and does not blurt out everything that is on her mind
Fights, argues and uses profanity in front of the kids	Always acts with respect and dignity particularly in front of her children
Has numerous men coming in and out of her home; random men have access to her children	Uses discretion with the men she chooses to have around her children
Gold digger who preys on men for the comfort and stability of herself and her children; lives a lavish lifestyle that she alone cannot afford; children wear the latest name brand clothes but barely can read and write	Understands that if she does not work, her nor her children will eat; she lives the lifestyle she can comfortably afford, children do well in school because she takes the time to help them be successful or finds others to help her help her children
Uses her body and sex as a means for provision and to further advance her career and lifestyle	Will rather use her brain to figure out a better way

This list is not exhaustive. There are far too many attributes that speak to dependency in so many different ways. Dependency is a mindset–a mindset that produces poverty. The same is true for the mindset of Independence–this mindset produces wealth.

It is absolutely vital for mothers and females with no children to know the difference. My objective is to increase the number of economic independent women in this world who approach life, love, and motherhood in a way that honors one another.

Wow! That is a lot to digest, but the differences between the dependent and independent woman are distinct. Let me tell you that I once had several attributes of my own definition of a dependent lifestyle and it was not a good look for me. It is not a good look for you or for any woman! Behaving like I did put me in a place of misery. I felt like my life was out of my control. I owe my life to the people who helped me realize where I needed improvement. Because they helped me gain a better understanding, I was able to change my life. Now I am here to help you do the same.

Don't be offended if you see that most or some of your current behavior places you in the dependent category; this just means that you have some work to do. Seeing where you are and where you want to be is the first step in creating lasting change in your life.

Whatever you do, don't be the female who can't handle the business affairs of being an independent woman because you refuse to put in the work and sacrifice to change destructive behaviors. The dependent lifestyle is a rat race with a dead end as the finish line.

The dependent lifestyle is a life of mental, physical, and spiritual suffering. Doing what is right for you won't be easy all of the time. Change is certainly not easy but making good decisions will make the difference between where you are and where you want to be. Remember–you are not just becoming a better woman for yourself; you are also doing it for your family.

Ladies, there is absolutely no reason why you should get caught with your back against the wall without a plan to change your life altogether. Wherever you are in life, start planning a better future and make the decision to start winning big today!

Remember, Independent Women use Wisdom, and Let their Light Shine. They Take on the Empire State of Mind, Have Heart and Stay Away from the Welfare Dependent Lifestyle!

CHAPTER SIX
Stronger

There is no way in the world I would be here today, if I had not confronted the spirit of fear. The truth of the matter is that you will not move from the place you stand if you are afraid of what lies before you. Becoming stronger is about exhibiting boldness and courage when facing the giants in your life. What are the giants in your life? Are they financial stability, relationships, hurt feelings, weight loss, obtaining your GED, getting past the experience of molestation, or obtaining a post-secondary education? No matter the giant, you will only defeat it as you move forward to fight it. Standing still in fear will keep you in the same place year after year.

Wars are won one battle at a time. Difficult situations exist to make you stronger, so get stronger! Facing difficult situations is a part of life and certainly a part of the life of purpose-driven people. There is no magic wand that one can waive to find success in life. Circumstances will knock you flat on your butt from time to time. When you fall, and you will fall–get back up and try again, again and again! Every battle you fight whether you win or lose is progress and a learning experience that will benefit you later in the journey of your life.

Don't try to fight the big giant with your current size and strength. It is bigger and stronger than you. Therefore, increase in stature (knowledge and wisdom) and position yourself for economic independence. The key to winning a war is to plan; take small steps and execute those steps with absolute commitment. These small steps are the small battles that you will need to win in order to win the bigger war. If you have not won, the smaller battles it will be impossible for you to win the war!

Don't forget to include your support team in all phases of your plan. The victorious ones never stand on the podium alone. You will need a good team to support you along your way.

Be strong in spite of criticism. "Nay Sayers" are those who seek to discredit and destroy your dreams. Have you ever been so excited about an idea and shared your idea with someone and they laughed at your idea? When they're finished, they simply leave you with a mess to clean up. The mess you are cleaning up is the one in your mind. You are now stuck fighting the negative thoughts and beliefs of others who were too scared to dream themselves or gave up at the first sign of failure.

If I listened to everyone who said I would never make it or that my ideas would never work, I would not be here today, and you would not be reading this book. I was simply tired of people who didn't have any dreams or aspirations telling me that my ideas would never work out. I had to realize that I was a different type of person. The nay-sayers and haters are nay-sayers and haters for a reason—because they have a limited view and often have no purpose in their own lives. Chances are they don't have any intention on working toward anything meaningful. Their aim is to bring you down to their level because they're more comfortable with who they are as long as you don't show them that they can be anything else.

There are people that will hate the standard that you have set for yourself. These people may be friends, family members, associates, rivals, enemies, or strangers. To find success, you will have to be comfortable with being despised, misunderstood, disliked and alone. Most people are uncomfortable with greatness and now that you are inspired to do great things, understand that this may make others feel pressure to strive for heights that they have yet committed to. You have to be comfortable with the idea that your dedication to success in life will start to make others uncomfortable. Be okay with this!

Many people have failed or stopped pursuing purpose simply because they have allowed others to annex their vision–whether through criticism, peer pressure, or intentional sabotage. Ladies, again I say, guard your heart and protect your vision at all cost. These people may appear to be friends, but they are enemies to your purpose. The farther you keep them away from you, the better off you will be. What you must do is keep them at a physical, mental, and spiritual distance. If you allow the light of your vision to be snuffed out by haters, it is your fault! They are doing what they are supposed to do and you will never be able to control what they do. The only thing you can control is how you respond to their type of negativity.

Will you endure to the end and fight the good fight of faith? Your ability to recognize when and where you are weak is critical. Partner with those who are strong in areas that you are not and understand that even strong people need someone to lean on.

Your purpose in life is inspired by God. Where you are weak, He is Strong! Always lean on Him.

Remember, Independent Women use Wisdom, and Let their Light Shine. They Take on the Empire State of Mind, Have Heart, Stay Away from the Welfare Dependent Lifestyle and Rely Not on Their Own Strength!

CHAPTER SEVEN

Let's Rock

Ladies let's rock! The time is now! Whether you are single with kids or married without kids, let's stand up and make a better life for ourselves now and for the future. Even if you are the woman who needs to make drastic changes in your life; your dreams are waiting on you! Make a commitment that you will start to be attentive to how you live your life and commit yourself to a path that will lead you to fulfilling your dreams. My goal is to help every young female become a R.E.A.L Woman–one who empowers herself through education, works to develop her gifts, looks to become the love she desires, demands the utmost respect, and is prepared to do whatever it takes to become that strong self-sufficient co-parent and leader. R.E.A.L. stands for Redefining Everything About Life and Love. Becoming a fully actualized R.E.A.L. Woman requires planning and follow-through.

I urge you to get busy being available to serve others who may be less or more fortunate than you. What you make happen for someone else, God will make happen for you. Serving others paves the way for God's blessings in your life. Being available for service will also keep your time busy and your mind on honoring the assignment of God for your life. Even if you are unsure about what your assignment and purpose is; acknowledge God in all your ways and he will direct your path.

Living for yourself is when you get up in the morning and all you think about is what you will wear, what you will eat, and how much of your day will go into pleasing and gratifying your own lustful desires. This ever-seeking and incomplete life is what lends to the constant need to fill voids. It's a life of constant emotional, mental, physical, and spiritual anguish. Eventually you'll get to the point where you will do anything to take your mind off the fact that you are empty without purpose or real love. You will make every attempt to numb the pain that emptiness creates. I urge you to begin filling that void by finding the time to serve others, for even the Son of Man did not come to be served, but to serve, and to give his life as a ransom for many. Doing this will help you connect to the needs of others and through compassion be fueled with a vision that will solve their problems. In essence, when you fix your feet upon paths that set out to help others–you help yourself.

Now for you ladies that may have children; I need for you to rock it out. Let's play the video tape to the end. Having children with little to no education, vision or purpose equals poverty and its many effects. The effects of poverty are the gateways to depression, poor mental and physical health, and possible thoughts of suicide–Real talk! Raising a child successfully is difficult enough with a husband;

it is vastly more difficult as a single mother. You will have to play superwoman– without any real superpowers. You cannot fly, nor can you run at the speed of light, read minds, shoot laser beams from your eyes, or bend cast iron bars with your bear hands. You will need a plan of action which will equip you with the resources and tools that empowers you to become financially independent so that you can provide a better quality of life for yourself and your children.

I would recommend seeking a degree, a professional certificate, or even multiple degrees if you have the stamina and desire. Find an academic or career field that you believe you are called to and enroll in the program that will teach and train you on all there is to know about your assignment.

Using myself as an example; I told myself for every child I had, I would obtain a degree. My first son I got my Associate's degree, the second son I obtained my Bachelor's, the third I acquired a Master's and the fourth son requires the Ph.D. law degree. Whether you want to become a nurse, public administrator, or photographer, once you start on your journey, do not stop until after you have crossed the finished line. Hence this is a lifetime of work, therefore be committed to a lifestyle where patience, peace and joy are present.

Let your field of study and the assignment on your life serve as the determining factors as to what kind of education and technical training you receive. One cannot fully serve their purpose without training or education. It is a mistake to think so. I see so many people who know what they have been called to do, yet they refuse to commit their time and energy to learning how to influence and make change in that arena. Study and master your craft is what I was told. If you are not willing to do what you are called to do with the spirit of excellence that supersedes the standard of the world, then simply don't bother.

If you are dependent upon various government programs for housing, utilities, medical insurance, food stamps, or child care vouchers, it is important to understand that these subsidies are temporary solutions to your financial situation. As soon as you get a job, these benefits are often cut. Welfare entitlements are designed to help those with low income. In order to continue receiving benefits you have to stay with low income. Many people never break their dependency on government subsidies because they choose to acclimate to that system and its sources of provision.

When you do the math, it does not take a rocket scientist to see that some benefit more by staying at home and not working just to keep the benefits. Let's keep it real ladies–these benefits such as housing, healthcare, food, and childcare are major–more like double major! I ask men, how on earth you can compete with a system that gives a woman all the necessities to life. I don't know that I would have been so determined to rid myself of welfare had it been comfortable for me. The fact is that it was very uncomfortable for me because I rarely qualified for assistance because I received child support.

I am however grateful for the Food-Stamp program which helped to feed my family. What was bothersome to me about having so many children was the fact that I could not afford them. The fact that I needed Food Stamps every month was something that I did not want to continue to need. Some people find themselves in a hard place, once or twice; while others live in that hard place for their entire life. I did not want to live in that place for the rest of my life and I sure as heck did not want to raise children in it.

I recall a conversation I had one day with a female and she told me that she got paid $1.16 an hour after she subtracted what she paid to get to and from work in addition to counting the loss of benefits she lost because she was working. It was substantially more beneficial to not work. However, the $1.16 an hour was the price she was willing to pay to keep her sanity and prevent from going into a depression. Working was helping her feel good about herself, and the only way that she thought she could get ahead. Ladies, if the mind is not right, nothing is right.

Now that's real, ladies... You have to understand that the welfare system is not designed to help you get ahead. To take advantage of their benefits you will have to stay impoverished. I urge you to look past welfare, public housing and section 8 as the source of your provision for the rest of your life. Having this perspective is critical if you want to travel the road of prosperity and purpose. Make plans that will empower you to become financially free and provide for you the life you dream of.

NOTE:

Financial aid and student loans are funds that social services do not count as income. In other words, you can use the educational system as the vehicle towards building that better life. Enrolling in school full time and maxing out your financial aid budget will bring you extra income that will help to take care of expenses that are incurred from being a full-time student (i.e. purchasing a new computer, child care, rent etc.).

I had a woman ask me one day over lunch, "Racquel do you think education is the only way out?" I said, "Yes, I do." She said, "What if I told you that it wasn't. Would you believe me?" I said nothing. She continued to say, "I believe that there is privilege, and then there is education." She also asked me, how many degrees I had. I said soon to be four. She said, "Wow!" "I have only a Bachelor's degree and do quite well for myself." Her job title and position were high as she led a huge department within state government. She expressed that her position was directly connected to her privilege and her family connections even though she had a college degree. She pointed out that even with my education it would have been difficult to advance to her position as a result of education alone.

Ladies, the moral of the story is there is privilege and there is education. If you were not born into a wealthy family, you should plan to work harder and educate yourself better than those with privilege just to make yourself competitive in today's job market. You will have to compete against individuals with more privilege and more advantage than you. This should not discourage you, however. Your ability to compete depends on your level of education, work ethic, and determination to succeed at whatever you set your goal to do.

Ladies if you do nothing else, use the information in this book to guide your decision making. Some of the lessons I had to learn were brutal to say the least. So brutal, there were times when my prayer was simply; Lord please help me get out of this mess with my right mind. I didn't want the end of my story to be one of tragedy or failure, because that was the path that I was heading on. Poverty and its effects were kicking my butt.

One day I did this exercise with my sons and showed them how much money it cost to provide the basic essentials for them. Then I calculated how much money I made over the years, the money that I received in child support and government subsidies that came into the house. I had a revelation. I was wowed by the fact that the greater provisions that sustained my family came from government subsidies. I looked at the Food Stamps, Medicaid and Child Care subsidies that I received for all of my children. It was scary to think that I was not at a point where I could afford to take care of my children on my own. It took me thirteen years to come out of that struggle.

I am confident that I would still be in that nightmare of a struggle had I not gone back to school. Ladies, obtaining a good education or technical job training is critical in determining how much money you will make over your lifetime. Please know that individuals who attend at least one year of post-secondary education earn over a million dollars more over the course of their lives than those who don't.

Let's Rock is a place where purpose and determination meet up. This is why I had to write to you. I had to let you know that you are beautiful and that you deserve the absolute best that life has to offer. I had to let you know that no matter where you are in life, you can achieve. No matter how poor you are, how undecided about what you want to do, or how many children you have, you can achieve whatever you want to achieve! I am a living example!

I have to warn you that achieving your dreams does not happen overnight. I have learned that not everyone has the same drive to thrive or the same patience and resilience to be successful. I am here to tell you that it will take all of these characteristics. I worked HARD to get where I am, and I work HARD every day to continue to progress on my life's plan.

Did you ever hear the phrase, "If you fail to plan, you plan to fail"? This statement couldn't be more accurate. Now the hard truth is that although you have a plan, it does not mean that 100% of the plan will play out according to your expectations. Life happens. Your planning is to keep you on track so that when life happens, you have a road map to get right back on the right path. Without a plan, you wouldn't know if you were going in the wrong direction–until, of course, it was too late. Know your path from a tumbleweed. If you want to do anything in life, you should have a plan to do it. Understand that the plans of man are many, but it is Gods will for your life that will prevail and find favor.

The 80/20 rule is critical in preparing for success. 80% of your time and effort should go into planning and twenty percent of your time used to implement or execute your plan. This ratio shows how important planning is. Before you do anything, it is important to have a clear and quality plan. This cannot be stressed enough!

Imagine a basketball team. About 80% of team time is spent practicing, working out, and strategizing even though the activities of the team are centered on performing for the game. The planning and preparation phase last much longer compared to execution phase.

Your plan should include a written action plan for what you will do, how you will do it, and how you will monitor how well you are doing according to the plan. You will need to divide your plans into phases. Breaking your plan into phases allows you to break your bigger plan into smaller parts. It is easier to see your plan develop as you accomplish each short-term goal along the way to accomplishing your ultimate long-term goals.

NOW is the best time to start planning your new life no matter where you are in life! Find a diary or planner that allows you to record your daily progress towards your goals in life.

You may be thinking that 10 years seems so long from now. The truth of the matter is hopefully in the next ten years you will be living; the question is how will you be living? Will you be struggling, hustling or living a thriving, vibrant life.

Having a plan for your life is a critical step in winning. Not a plan that will sit on a bookshelf; but a plan that will be hung up on your wall like a photo. I recommend getting a cork board and turning it into your vision board. On this board you will stick photos of your dream school, career, home, car, husband, yacht, business, and use your planner to provide a step by step breakdown of what you will need to accomplish in order to manifest the vision you have set your heart upon. Whatever will keep you connected to your vision is what you must have in front of you every day. It's like the old saying goes; out of sight–out of mind. It is the things we keep before our eye and ear gate that will enter into our hearts.

In your planning, acknowledge God in all your ways and he will direct your path. Believe that your footsteps are ordered. He is on your side contrary to what you may believe. God says that the plans of man are many, but it is His will for your life that will prevail. It is His plan for your life that will be given victory and win favor above all the plans that you have for yourself. Trust in the Lord with all your heart and mind and watch your new life unfold right before your very eyes.

Remember, Independent Women use Wisdom, and Let their Light Shine. They Take on the Empire State of Mind, Have Heart, Stay Away from the Welfare Dependent Lifestyle, Rely Not on Their Own Strength and Rock Out the Plans for Their Lives.

CHAPTER EIGHT
The Blueprint

Have you ever read or heard the story of the Underground Railroad? Harriet Tubman had a system that worked. There were no actual railroads running underground. The Underground Railroad consisted of homes, rest stops, horse carts and other traveling mechanisms that would take slaves from one place to the other. Coded languages were used to alert others on this "railroad system" when a package was to arrive. Consider this chapter in the same context. Listen, I made it out to freedom; mental freedom, economic freedom and spiritual freedom that has afforded me the freedom to help others. Therefore, I have been charged to go back and direct women like you to do the same. On Harriet's railroad to freedom, you could not change the route. She knew the route, she could communicate with the human assets within the system, and she knew what worked and the best times to travel.

The Blueprint to success is your underground railroad. It is centered on the one thing that will permanently advance your ability to become the woman of your dreams–education. The beauty of it all is that this railroad is not underground. It is a well-known fact that education is critical to economic empowerment and quality of life. The problem is that many of us don't realize it until it is too late.

More and more people, no matter where they are in life, are looking to advance their education to become economically empowered and independent. In today's economy, manufacturing careers are constantly decreasing. The nation's economy and competitive job market warrants that individuals obtain an educational degree, professional licensure, technical certification or training in a highly specialized skill. Your skills should be matured and developed to the degree that it adds value to people's lives; whereas you can exchange your skills in the marketplace for money.

Does this mean that once you have a good education, you will automatically have a good job? Not necessarily. There are millions of educated people who are out of work. Education is key to your success but understand that even with education you will still have to work hard and constantly pursue purpose and the assignment for your life.

Please hear me when I say that this education railroad is not just so that you can get a good job and make a lot of money, although that is very relevant to your quality of life. Education is central to who you are and what you are called to do. The key is how you use education to develop your gifts and increase your skills in the fervent pursuit to manifest your God given assignment here on earth. Education is central to who you are, what you are called to do, how you will develop your gifts, acquire more knowledge and increase your skills in a fervent pursuit to manifest your God given assignment here in the earth. I call education the Underground Railroad because it is the surest way to obtain financial self-sufficiency and unleash the realm of creativity that lies within you. It helps you develop skills such as critical thinking–a skill vital to problem solving. Education is the vehicle that you can use to fulfill your dreams and change your life.

For my sisters who receive government assistance, pursuing an education will help you advance your earning potential dramatically, freeing you from the clutches of poverty or entitlement dependency. While it may be easy to sit back and rely on the government, your quality of life and self-confidence will be multiplied when you are able to earn a higher income and build wealth.

My coming through on the other side was for you. I never gave up and in turn God used my pain to fuel my passion. I had to succeed; for failure was not an option. Did I fail? Many times, but I never took defeat as the final answer. It was all worth it ladies–

every tear, every prayer and lesson learned! I knew then, it was all about you. I went through my journey specifically with you in mind. I made that promise to God–If he helped me keep my sanity and I will surrender my life to helping His people. He has kept His side of the deal and now I am keeping mine. So, because I have made it through, I am here to tell you to pack your bags because we are going to the other side.

If you stay with me, your life will be transformed, and you will be able to one day live a life you've only dreamed of living. I need for you to commit yourself to the entire contents of this book; read over and over again if and when necessary.

Although education is central to economic advancement, you will also need to pay attention to the personal changes that you will need to make in order to grow and develop into the Real Woman. Personal development and character will take you places money cannot. Without character, the plan is cracked and bound to break. This transformation will not happen overnight. In fact, it will take quite a bit of time, but that time depends on you. It depends on your desire to want something better and your relentless non-stop work ethic. If you are lazy, beloved, you will die in the wilderness.

This simple blueprint will guide you to become the woman of your dreams if you follow it. The Blueprint will work whether you have no kids, one child or many children. The Blueprint consists of 6 points:

BLUEPRINT #1: GET A GOOD EDUCATION

First and foremost, there is a direct correlation between income and educational attainment. The more education you have, the more money you will make. Income is also directly correlated with physical health, mental health, social involvement, and community service. Family income is also directly related to academic performance of children. The higher family income is, the higher the child's grades and test scores. The more education you attain, the better your quality of life is, and the brighter your children's futures will be.

This is no joke ladies. Education is absolutely central to a better way of life. It will open doors for you and empower you to help yourself and others. It will validate you as a professional in your field of study. Although it is not an end all be all solution, not having a good education is not an option when you are trying to escape poverty and its effects.

If you have no high school diploma, go back to school to obtain your General Education Diploma (GED). Your high school diploma or GED is critical to moving you to accreditation towards a professional career. Think of this step as the game of monopoly. You cannot collect the big bucks until you pass "Go" the first time. Your diploma or GED is the starting point for preparing your future. Once you have earned your high school diploma or GED you become eligible for post-secondary education and training. Once you get past that point there are a number of scholarships, grants, and financial aid options available for you to continue your education.

If you are currently in school and you are pregnant, DO NOT DROP OUT! Without a diploma or GED, it is not likely that you will be able to work to get ahead. There are very few jobs that will pay you enough to become free from government assistance and dependency on others. The more children you have the more that will be required of you to become self-reliant.

If you are in high school, you should be in the guidance counselor's office seeking help with college applications and admission processes into universities that offer what you are interested in pursuing. There is no excuse in waiting until your guidance counselor comes to you, be aggressive in your pursuit and go to them for help first. If you have been out of school for some time, then my advice to you is start at the community college level and move forward from there.

Educational institutions are like the safe houses Harriet Tubman used to take slaves to freedom. They are designed to educate the public so that people would be able to add and contribute in various ways to the greater whole of society. For the most part, educators who work within these institutions are there because they believe that knowledge is power, and they want to see you become powerful. They often hold the golden keys to the next level in your life. Every major door that I went through was a direct result of an educator's words and or deeds.

I want you to look at the educational system as the main pipeline to freedom. There are limitless opportunities within the educational system. Each door can take you on a different path anywhere and I mean anywhere. For example, you can travel the world through various types of student exchange programs that will afford you the opportunity to visit and learn from other cultures and ethnic groups. This exposure looks great on your resume and broadens your mind to a world that is bigger than your block or neighborhood. It was through this system that I was afforded the opportunity to visit Liberia for two weeks. One of my sons was awarded an all-expense paid trip to China. These are the opportunities that educational institutions will bring right to your feet. It is only ignorance and fear that will keep you from taking advantage of them.

Educational institutions provide inroads to your career like internships in various corporate or government settings; opportunities that you may not have been afforded if you were not a part of these educational institutions.

I cannot begin to tell you the blessings that came from my attending college. The doors that were opened to me, the advice and relationships that were built are absolutely priceless. There is no amount of money I would exchange for any of the many opportunities and relationships that I was able to establish and grow.

Did I find purpose in school, NO! Purpose found me and pushed me towards the paths of higher education. It was higher education that taught me how to use my skills and talents to make change in the area I was called to influence. It was my experiences that equipped me with the tools to make sense of how my purpose will play out and manifest in the earth.

Okay, did I beat that horse until it was dead? You got it! I'm pretty sure I will mention the words education at least ten more times before the book is over. I will not apologize for that. There are no words that I can use to stress to you how important this is.

BLUEPRINT #2: PICK THE RIGHT SCHOOL FOR YOU

There is a wide variety of educational institutions that you can choose from; job training programs, 2-year community colleges, 4-year and online universities are all viable choices to excel your academic goals. You will also have the choice between private and public institutions. Where you decide to enroll should depend on how much you want to pay for school, what career field you want to pursue and where you want to enroll in school. Choosing the right school is very important. After you have decided what you want to study, how much you want to pay, what you want to do, and where you want to go, you can begin to decide what institution and program is right for you. Some institutions are preferred over others in terms of the programs and support services they offer.

Private schools often offer a superior education, but at a much higher price than public institutions. Though they are more expensive than public institutions, depending on scholarships, savings, field of study, or the particular talents you plan to develop, a private school may be the right choice for you.

Public colleges and universities also offer quality education and at a lower price than private institutions. Choosing a state school may benefit you financially in the long term. Tuition is lower, thus more loan money may be available for investing in long-term capital and resources that increase your net worth and ability to earn more.

BLUEPRINT #3: SPEND REFUND MONEY WISELY

Student loans are a form of financial aid and are guaranteed as long as you are a full-time student, meet academic requirements, in good standing with past student loans, and have not been convicted of drug related charges while receiving financial aid. The one thing you never want to do is default on your student loan. Default is when you fail to make your loan payments. Never, and I mean never, default on your student loans. I am not advocating that you acquire huge amounts of debt. I am suggesting that even your academic goals be strategic and a means to get you where you need to be. If you cannot afford school, the government has made a way to do so. I'll ask you this question: If someone was to offer you a low interest loan that you would not have to pay back until you completed what you set out to complete and all that was required of you was writing papers, taking test and studying; would you apply for the loan? I think most of you would. There was a time in my life when school was my job– this is what some call a professional student. However, I purposed in my heart that I would never allow for my student loans to default and when it was time to pay them pack; I would be in a position to do so and not be broke.

There is still hope if you have a student loan in default. You should call your debtor and let them know you are looking to bring the account out of default. They will grant you the opportunity to make a payment arrangement of at minimum fifty ($50) dollars a month for six (6) consecutive months. This minimum amount may vary from person to person. Once you have made the required payments, your account will be brought out of default and placed in a forbearance status. You can then begin to receive student loans to help you with school and related expenses.

Spend refund money on sustaining where you are and preparing for where you want to go. The smartest uses of refund money include paying rent, buying a house, buying a car, purchasing computer equipment, buying software, or purchasing any other form of capital asset that you may need to start a business or build wealth.

Every time I received my refund, I would pay off my rent for six (6) months at a time and while I was in school, I did not have the pressures of raising my four sons and paying bills. I was able to focus on my education and being a better mother. Because of this I graduated top of my class all the time. I received higher grades than most people in my class who had no children.

Please note that failure to maintain adequate grades will result in financial aid probation and eventually a total loss of your aid. I say all this to let you know that this is not the time to make poor decisions. It is the time to put your action plan in fifth gear.

I have known many people to go through the process of getting admitted into school only to withdraw once they receive their refund. Some students lose their minds in stores buying things that they don't need. This is absolutely foolish. You should focus on making purchases that increase your wealth and advance your personal and professional goals.

Remember, this is borrowed money that you will have to pay back. Some of the worst uses of refund money consist of going out to the clubs, buying bottles of expensive wine, clothes, hair, nails, tattoos, and any other superficial purchases that will not last or advance you in any way. Also, just say "no" to the many people who will come to you to beg, borrow, and steal. Have a purpose for your money and don't get away from that purpose for any reason. Stay focused ladies! Throwing your money down the drain and forsaking your priorities is almost criminal at this point of your life. Be smart. Becoming the Real Woman is a long road. Don't be your own roadblock.

NOTE:

If you are receiving public assistance; student loans and financial aid are not considered reportable income. This means that you do not have to inform your caseworker that you are receiving financial aid, unless they ask; and in all cases they will not count it as income. This allows a little pressure to be alleviated off of you. In fact, most government programs will allow you to continue to pursue at least an Associate's degree and in most cases a bachelor's degree.

Most states will also pay for childcare if you are enrolled in school at least part time and work at least part-time. I say this to say that there are opportunities for you to advance your life no matter where you are. It is important for you to take the initiative to get an education, work, and make it your business to change your life around. While there are support systems that will help you along the way, no one can or will do the work for you.

BLUEPRINT #4: DELAY INSTANT GRATIFICATION (D.I.G.)

D.I.G. deep within yourself to postpone, delay, defer, put off, or prolong moments of satisfaction in order to prevent situations that will harm you in the long run. Instant gratification is the sure road to long-lasting disaster. What seems "right" at the moment often proves to make us cry later. In many cases cry for years. Whether its unprotected sex, bad relationships, or poor choices; the cost of a mistake due to a lack of discipline could mean a horrifying reality in the future. Unprotected sex can lead to incurable sexually transmitted diseases, HIV and unwanted pregnancies!

Please, ladies present your bodies as a living sacrifice holy and acceptable unto the Lord. This is hard and only real women can employ such discipline. When physical desires are gratified immediately, it is often done with no planning or regard for future consequences, and because of this recklessness, bad things happen as a result. To delay instant gratification means to defeat temptation. Learning to say "no" will take you a long way toward avoiding drug abuse and postponing children until you are married and ready to start a family.

If you delay instant gratification for five minutes at a time, you would have delayed it for an hour. Delaying it for an hour turns into two hours. Eventually the time delayed will add up to twelve and twenty-four hours. Sometimes, the only thing that stands between a really dumb decision and a really good decision is TIME!

The other thing that will help you fight temptation is SPACE. Keep negative influences away from you and stay away from situations that may tempt you. Keep the negativity at a distance and it will be practically impossible for it to intrude in your thoughts. The temptations of drugs and sex are greatly reduced when you don't allow drugs or people who do drugs around you. It is easier to avoid sex when you don't put yourself in a position where it is possible for you to have sex. Remember, misery loves company. Be careful of the company you keep. Let's not forget productivity. The more productive you are, the less time you will have to get into counter- productive activities.

Whatever the temptation, play the tape all the way to the end. In other words, fast forward and determine what could happen as a result of you making this poor decision. If the end is not positive; press pause or even stop. Start all over by getting space and time between you and the temptation. While you have separated from the scene, pondering on the tempting thoughts will only have you replay the scene all over again. At all cost you must immediately think on other things.

BLUEPRINT #5: WAIT FOR LOVE

The Bible tells us to wait for love until it so desires. Love requires a mature heart. Wait for Love, daughters! Understanding what love is and isn't should come first in our lives. Often, we jump head first into relationships that are built on lust and admiration, but totally devoid of love. Relationships can be dangerous when they are not built on true love.

Remember love is patient and kind. It does not envy, it does not boast, it is not proud. It does not dishonor others, it is not self-seeking, not easily angered, and keeps no record of wrongs. Love does not delight in evil but rejoices with the truth. It always protects, always trusts, always hopes, and always perseveres.

False love shows up in the form of jealousy, control, abuse, and insecurity. This is the place where you are least protected and full of fear, worry, doubt and insecurity. When these demons show their face in a relationship, know that the relationship is poisonous and could very well compound problems in your life. Love is vital to the abundant life. We all need love; however, we need real love. Ladies, we have to be ready to rid ourselves of the poison which masquerades in the form of love. It is when we become Real Women, we are able to easily detect and reject counterfeits.

Real love starts from within. Love yourself first. Meditate on what love is and begin to display the characteristics of love in your daily life. Until, your heart is mature and ready to give love what it demands, you should wait for love. After all, love waits patiently for you.

BLUEPRINT #6: CREATE A STRONG SUPPORT SYSTEM

First of all, let's define support system. **Support** means to maintain or serve as a foundation by supplying it with things necessary for existence. A **system** is a group of persons or things forming a complex whole. Although we may use these words throughout our everyday lives, it is important to define the words to get a clearer understanding in terms of how to apply every facet of the word to our daily decision-making as it pertains to choosing the right system and the right people to flow in our system. Support systems are crucial if not absolutely mandatory for you to find success in life, especially if you are a single mother.

Support systems are not built overnight. They take months and years to become rock solid and must be flexible to adapt to sudden change. You should have individuals in your life that support your personal, academic, and professional endeavors. Single mothers, you should have people that help you in the day to day tasks that make your life easier and free you up to take care of your responsibilities outside of the home. These people also free you up to take much needed mental health breaks. You should have people in your system who guide your personal development (mind, body and spirit). You should have people in your life that guide your spiritual development. You should have people in your life that monitor your academic performance and development. You should also have people that you talk to and trust–to guide your professional development.

Sometimes individuals in your support system have to be replaced or repositioned. There will be times when individuals in your support system will turn their backs on you, pull the rug from underneath your feet and straight up stab you in your back. These are called distractions. Depending on the role an individual plays in your support system determines whether or not it is a minor or major distraction.

Distractions draw your attention away from what is most important. No matter how big or small a distraction may be; it is only a temporary circumstance. Be ready to move on and make changes in your support system whenever and wherever necessary. Keeping this in mind will help you easily get back on track and help you maintain your focus. When you have a vision, there will be all types of people and circumstances that will attempt to block you from reaching your goal in life.

Support systems are not automatic; they require strategic planning. Support systems are designed to hold you down mentally, emotionally, spiritually and physically. The individuals who serve in your system could be family, friends, colleagues, and elders who have the desire, ability, and commitment to mentor or help you where you need help. Someone who acts as a mental support for you should be someone who is mentally stable and has experience in acting in this role. They should be mentally strong and able to support you as you travel down the path toward manifesting your vision. The same goes for academic, spiritual, and professional support. People who support you in these areas should be capable and proven professionals or adults. Ability is very important. Whatever role an individual play in your support system, they should have proven themselves to operate well within that given capacity; allowing individuals who are incompetent to support you is likely to compound your problems and make your journey more difficult.

When searching for people to provide support in your life journey, seek people who are proven. Ask them for their help and tell them exactly what you need them to do. Be open to their criticism and advice. If you seek academic help, let your potential mentor know what you are trying to accomplish and that you need them to hold you accountable for doing the things that will help you achieve your goals. If spiritual support, ask your spiritual mentor to monitor your actions to make sure they are in line with the principals that you want to live by. This Spiritual advisor should have mastered areas of their life that you are looking to overcome. If professional support, ask your mentor to help guide you along your career path and hold you accountable to the things you will need to do to achieve your career goals.

The amount of people needed in your support system will vary from person to person. Support systems exist to support direct activities and actions associated with the execution and implementation phase of your plan. Make sure they are the right people to work with. Make sure these people have a genuine interest in helping you with no strings attached and that they are committed to the work it will take to help you to the finish line. Make sure they are quality people with characteristics that you aspire to acquire. Make sure they are people with integrity; people that are responsible; and people that are successful at what they do; for these are the characteristics that you want to become synonymous with who you are as a person.

Integrity is marked by one's moral and ethical principles. It is marked by honesty. Because you seek to be a person with integrity, it is important to work with others who have integrity. There is no honor amongst thieves or those who lack integrity. Integrity is what drives us to be fair and just. Great leaders are those who have a high regard for honesty. For you to find the success that you seek, you will need to exemplify the same integrity that you seek in your mentors.

Seek individuals who are responsible. What you are asking of them requires work. They will be asked to hold you accountable for accomplishing your goals; which implies they are great with setting goals and accomplishing them. They have a life that looks accomplished. Remember you have a support system because you need the help of others to carry out important functions. When these functions are not carried out, this can result in serious, delays in your plan.

In your relationship with your mentors and support system, you should also seek to be accountable to them. You will need to be responsible in communicating with your support system and doing everything that you say you will do. Being dependable yourself is just as important as seeking dependable people to be a part of your support system.

While you are plugging people into your super support system, understand that they are sewing their time and talents into your life to help you. Just as you have expectations of them, you should live up to their expectations of you. Make sure you are where you say you will be and do what you say you will do. This will help others trust you and bend over backwards for you when times get tough. Whether it's your professor, professional mentor, pastor, or babysitter; when people trust you, they will support you and invest more and more into you.

Make sure that you choose mentors who are successful at what they do. You want their success to rub off on you. Choosing people who are unsuccessful at what they do is like infusing failure into your support system. Choose people to play a part in your support system that have attributes that you admire and respect. Leaders often dictate the altitude that an organization will reach in terms of success, and so it is with your support team. Your ability to reach your goals will have a direct correlation with the type of people you choose to be a part of your support system.

BLUEPRINT #7: SERVE GOD WITH ALL YOUR MIGHT

I saved the best rule for last. Love the Lord your God with all you your heart and with all your soul, and with all your strength and with your entire mind; and Love your neighbor as yourself[19].

19 Luke 10:27. The Holy Bible

Remember, your inspiration comes from God. Your purpose and destiny in life come from God. All of your blessings come from God. All of your talents, gifts, and abilities come from God. In the course of becoming a Real Woman always, and I mean always, keep God first in your life. Allow the Lord to be the lamp unto your feet and the light unto your path and you will never go wrong. He will lead you in the right direction and never lead you astray. He will never leave you alone on this special and unique journey called life. You may be uncertain as to the specifics of what your future holds, just make it your business to know the One who holds your future. He is the Great I AM and you are the apple of His eye.

Now that you have access to the all that it takes to become the woman of your dreams, all you have to do now is DREAM! Dream out loud, dream with vivid colors and dream the most outrageous dream. Dreams become a reality when we are equipped with the right tools. The skills that you were given in this book will help you manage the greatness that the dream alive will bring. Your destiny awaits you! Find it and go for it full throttle!

Thank you for reading this book! I love you! Great things are meant to be shared. Recommend or pass this book along to a friend and take the journey together. Be blessed and never stop working toward becoming an Independent Woman relying on your GOD and the purpose for which you have been called to fulfill.

Remember, Independent Women use Wisdom, and Let their Light Shine. They Take on the Empire State of Mind, Have Heart, Stay Away from the Welfare Dependent Lifestyle, Rely Not on Their Own Strength, Rock Out the Plans for Their Lives, Learn from the Mistakes of Others and Follow those Who Model the Way!

Until next time!

ACKNOWLEDGEMENT
Can I Live, Inc.

Can I Live, Incorporated (CIL-INC) is a 501(c)3 national tax-exempt nonprofit agency dedicated to reducing dependency on government subsidies for HUD-assisted families. Through the pathways of education and entrepreneurship, we advance affordable housing, economic inclusion, and personal responsibility. We are building an inclusive society, where all people can build powerful lives centered around great health and economic empowerment.

History

Founded in 2005 in New York, Can I Live, Inc., began its footsteps as an advocacy agency promoting affordable housing for single mothers. A petition called the Single Mothers Cry for Help was the beginning of the agency's movement to improve the quality of life for women living in poverty. Divinely inspired to make a difference in the lives of people struggling with becoming self-reliant; founder Racquel Williams-Jones (RW Jones), decided to accept her life's purpose to help others ask the question—"Can I Live?" with a resounding YES by holding people accountable and helping them take personal responsibility for the decisions they make.

Headquartered in the Nation's Capital (Washington, DC), Can I Live continues to bring innovation that ignites low-income communities to action.

Support the
One Million Moms
Off Welfare™
(1MMOW Iniative)

We believe that, all Americans are created equal and possessed of inalienable rights to life, liberty, the pursuit of happiness—and to justice under the law. Yet the entitlements provided to millions of moms living at or below poverty are structured to keep them poor while entitlements offered to wealthier Americans and corporations assist in wealth creation and prosperity. We don't want Welfare…We Want WEALTHFAIR!

CanⓘLive
Bringing Opportunity Home
www.canilive.org

Racquel Williams-Jones

The author of the Hands-On book collection which includes: Get Your Hands Out My Pocket: The Hands-On Guide to Avoiding the Child Support System and Get Your Hands Off My Butt: The Hands-On Guide to Avoiding the Welfare System.

RW Jones, uses her personal challenges and triumphs to teach personal development, communication and the importance of maintaining healthy relationships.

CanᒫLive
Bringing Opportunity Home
www.canilive.org

Visit Our website to learn more about products and services offered by Can I Live, Inc.

Made in the USA
Middletown, DE
23 June 2023

33301842R00076